21 Habit Building Techniques: How to Transform your Life in Thirty Days .

I0421994

By James Woods

Table of Contents

Introduction

"We are what we repeatedly do. Excellence, then, is not an act, but a habit." -Aristotle

As children, we are taught to aim for the best, do our very best, and succeed. The attainment of success is ever imprinted in our minds. We all strive to succeed from a young age until the day we die. We are taught from a tender age that education and hardwork is the fomula to success, yet few ever achieve such success. We then need to question if education and hardwork is enough for one to succeed at anything in life. In theory, education and hardwork can make us successful, but this success is limited to our studies. What many people aim for is success in life.

What, then, is success? The English dictionary defines success as simply an "accomplishmet of an aim or purpose." Defining success in real life circumstances, however, is not simple. A lot of people dont know whether they are successful or not. The problem with our society is that it looks at success in the wrong way. Success is defined and measured poorly, which is at the core of the problem. The bar of achieving success is set up way too high, and beyond the reach of many. The "success bar", as I like to refer to it, is the billionare businessman, the multibillion dollar business cooperation, the world famous football player, and many others who, in the eyes of the world, have attained the imposible. We all endeavour to follow the footsteps of those who have succeeded and laid the path for us.

Success is all about reaching individul goals. It is not about what others before you have done. It is important to realize that those who are successful had their time and did their best with it, and now it is your time. Success is all about you and no one else; draw inspiration from those who have already succeeded, but do not try to be them. Be you, and set the bar which you alone can reach. There is a very thin line that seperates succes and competitiveness, but it is easy to become destracted along the road to success, and you find yourself competing instead of succeeding. There once was a man who set out to run just a few blocks around his neighborhood, and when he was just about to get to the finish line, he saw the person who was ahead of him. He forgot about the finish line for his race and started a new one; competing with the man that was ahead of him. He raced the man until he had passed him, and carried on racing everyone that was ahead of him. He eventually became so exhausted and stopped running, and was surprised to find himself in the middle of nowhere. He had ran many miles instead of a couple of blocks.

Success is running your own race and achieving your goals. Running a few blocks from your house is success because that is your goal and what you set out to achieve.

Many of us forget this, and we think success is about being better than others. We become so competitive that we forget ourselves and what we really want out of life. The man in the story forgot too quickly that he just wanted to run a few blocks to blow off steam. He started to compete in a marathon race of his own, which he was not prepared for.

When you begin to realize that success is all about you, it is no longer hard to define nor is its attainment out of reach. Success is what you make of it. Simply put, success is a habit. Success, then, becomes a mere routine of attaining our goals and fulfilling our aim and purpose in life. Our habits make us who we are. Good habits make us better people, and bad habits are our downfall. Understanding our habits is the only way we can tranform our lives for the better and become success stories. Generally speaking, there is no normal person who wants to be identified as a failure. There is no sane person who sets out to become an alcoholic, drug adict, school dropout, or set out to become unhappy. The predicaments that we at times find ourselves in, are a result of a series of our own actions. A lot of people always try to shift the blame of their failures onto other people or the outside environment.

Alcoholism, drug addiction, and obesity are a result of an uncontrollable habit. The craving for alcohol, drugs, and food comes from within a person, although there are outside factors which may contribute. Far too many people make the mistake of blaming their bad addictions on factors like rejection, bad childhood, or abuse as being the major contributing factors to their problems. A problem can only be diagnosed and treated at its source.

Building up good habits is integral to our success in life. Bad habits are like a noose around our necks, if we choose to be enslaved by them. If we make the choice of substituting every bad habit we have for a good habit, we can transform our lives in an unimaginable way. For example, if someone quits smoking and substitutes this bad habit with a good habit of excercising, they make a difference and may have added years to their lifespan. Think about how many good things you can accomplish if you would get over the habit of spending most of your time sitting on a couch watching television. There are a lot of people who never get to achieve anything in life, yet alone get around to do even the smallest of tasks because they are slaves to their own bad habits. If you are a slave to television, a simple task like cleaning your room becomes difficult to accomplish. For every bad habit you have under your sleeve, know that it keeps you from something that is actually good for you. Biting your nails keeps you from having beautiful nails. In the same way, drinking excessive amounts of alcohol keeps you from having a healthy liver. For every bad habit that you keep, you prevent something good from prevailing in your life. Bad habits undermine you and they prevent you from achieving your goals.

Good habits are our stepping stones to successs whereas bad habits are stumbling blocks. The greatest power comes from within, and with it we can tranform our lives. Habits make us who we are, and our transformation takes place when we change these habits, but to change what you cannot comprehend is a futile exercise. We need to first and foremost understand how habits come into being.

Chapter 2 Habit 1-7

1. Commit Yourself

Dedication is the key to building good habits. If you want to transform your life in the most positive way, the first step you need to take is in committing yourself to the task at hand. Do not simply be involved; you must commit wholeheartedly to transforming yourself in thirty days. It is of large importance that you understand that you have reached a turning point, and you have the opportunity to alter your life. Understand what needs to be done and give it your all. To be able to fully commit to something, you need to understand the importance of the thing you wish to commit to, and what is at stake.

If you want to transform your life in thirty days, the first step you need to take is to commit yourself to the objective. Look at the big picture; you want to transform your life for the better, but you have bad habits that hold you back, and you wish to build good habits that can make you successful at anything in life. Just saying it is not enough. You need to live by your commitment and be prepared to make a sacrifice.

You need to understand what it means to fully commit to something. You need to give this exercise a 110% effort. Be prepared to make sacrifices and understand that what you sacrifice is for the greater good. Letting go of bad habits enables you to develop good habits that are important and necessary to achieving your goals. You cannot prevail at anything without total commitment on your part. To fully commit to this transformation, you need to put this exercise at the top of your list. It is impossible to commit to something without first making it a priority. If building good habits is important to you, there is absolutely nothing that can stop you from committing yourself to the objective.

State the objective on paper or mark it on your calendar the date you begin the exercise, and put it on display in a prominent place. It will make it easier to uphold your commitment if there is a constant reminder. For instance, if you wish to make drinking water your regular habit, you need to write this on a piece of paper and stick it on to your refrigerator door. Each time you open the refrigerator to take something, you are reminded of what you committed to, making it easier to reach for the water instead of reaching for a soda, because it is what you committed to.

2. Know That You Can Change

The second step in transforming your life lies in acknowledging that you have the power. No one can change you or transform you to perfection. That ability is in your grasp alone. A lot of people go through life thinking they cannot change; they feel and act like rejects because it is in their mind that they were born like that and cannot change because it is whom they are.

If you do not like who or how you are, then choose not to be that person. It is not healthy for you, or anyone, to go on loathing yourself and disliking the person who stares back at you when you look in the mirror. Life is about choices. It is your choice whether to transform or not. The biggest challenge many individuals face in transforming themselves is that they do it to please people. When you transform yourself to please another person, you are simply engaging in a charade, and as far as charades go, soon or later you are going to have to give up the act. It is like when you go on a weight loss program because your husband says you have gained weight. While the weight loss program gives you the desired result, the motivation to continue staying healthy is not coming from you; it comes from your husband and your need to please him. What then happens when he is not there to keep you motivated? What happens when he does not notice all your efforts to please him? The end result is that you will slip into your own cocoon of depression and all your efforts will be reversed. However, if you go on a weight loss program for yourself because you want to feel and look good for you, you will more than likely be successful. You will be able to maintain the result of the weight loss because it is your achievement, which you are proud of, and the motivation to live a healthy lifestyle is coming from within yourself. The power to transform comes from within, and with it we can transform and break free from bad habits.

If you blame your alcohol abuse on a past experience, like a bad childhood or rejection, you will not be able to break free of the habit because you are giving up control and power to this habit to your past. By doing this, you are saying that in order for you to break free from this habit your past must change. The reality of the matter is that no one can travel back in time and alter their misfortune or negative experience. The problem is that when we blame our past for our present predicaments, we remove ourselves from the equation and we simply focus on our negative experiences as the only contributing factor to our problems and never acknowledge the part we play in causing dysfunction in our own lives. Focusing on our past renders us useless and disables us of the power to change. If you blame a bad childhood for your alcohol abuse, it means that there is nothing you can do about it,. You cannot stop something that has already happened. When you fail to recognize your power, you give away your willpower, and without willpower you cannot change. In the end, you will carry on abusing alcohol. It is different, however, when we confront our past and try to heal and move on. When we move on, we live in the present and are conscious of our decisions. The power we have is limitless and it gives us the power of choice. We are able to choose the good habits we need to move forward.

3. Get to Know Your Habits

We cannot break free from bad habits if we don't identify them as bad habits. You need to take a look at your life and the way you live. Ask yourself pertinent questions, like: Am I leading a healthy lifestyle? Do I like the way my life has turned out? Am I proud of the way I live? Am I on the right track to achieving my dreams? Asking yourself such questions helps you in understanding yourself. Your habits, both good and bad, make you who you are.

The challenge that many people have is that they do not know their habits. It is only when someone points it out to them that they can become aware of its existence. A habit is an automatic routine that you do almost subconsciously. How, then, can you evaluate your habits if you do not know them yourself? The answer is in making a diary; diarize everything you do from the moment you wake up to the moment you go to bed. This might seem like a petty exercise, but it is necessary in making you understand your lifestyle and, in turn, your habits. For you to be able to recognize a habit, you need to carry out this exercise for at least a week, and then you will be able to notice a pattern. A habit is that which you do every day or more frequently in a single day.

The next stage involves making a list of your habits. On one side, list all of your good habits, and on the other side, list all of your bad habits. Good habits add value to your life whilst bad habits do exactly the opposite. Putting your habits on paper can be life changing, because your lifestyle is spelled out in explicit detail before your eyes. In that moment, you have to make a choice to either change or continue living the way you have been living. Listing your habits helps to make a decision on which habits you should keep and which ones you should let go of. This will be the easiest part of the exercise; identifying the habits you should keep; good habits stay and bad habits go.

Old habits are hard to break. It is not easy to let go of something you have become accustomed to. For you to let go of a bad habit, making a resolution to change may not be enough. You might need to understand the habit before you start making resolutions. If you understand the habit and try to recall what might have brought it on, then you can become more equipped to deal with the habit. For example, you may want to stop drinking alcohol every night. Making a resolution to stop drinking is not enough. The problem that needs to be tackled first, before getting to the drinking part, is establishing the cause. One needs to identify the reason behind the drinking. Pressure at work may be the cause to your drinking or boredom. So, rather than simply stating that "I am going to stop drinking," tackle the source of the problem. If pressure at work is making you drink, consider looking for another job, or approach your supervisor and state your grievance. Similarly, if boredom is the cause of your drinking, then it is time for you to find new hobbies that are healthy for you.

In order for one to understand their habits, they need to use the habit formation model. The first thing you do is identify the habit. After identification, locate the cue, so as to understand the trigger that makes you behave that way. The reward is ease of recognition, and with that knowledge one will be able to fully comprehend what they are dealing with.

4. Take Responsibility

Once you have identified your bad habits, it is important that you take responsibility. Quit blaming others or situations as the cause for your bad habits. It is your life, and you are the only person able to control the direction your life takes. When you blame others, you give up that control and you cannot move forward. When you take responsibility for your actions, it means you accept and acknowledge your failings. Taking responsibility enables you to stop making excuses, which is a major deterrent when giving up bad habits. The reason why it is so hard for you to give up a bad habit is because you are always making excuses. It is hard to quit a bad habit like smoking if you are always on the defensive and you constantly say, "What can I do, I can't help it".

If you are not meeting your targets at work, do not blame others for that. Take responsibility and acknowledge your failure. Accepting responsibility is not a weakness; it is power, which gives you the strength to face the problem head on. If you take responsibility for not being able to meet your targets at work, you will be able to evaluate your performance and identify any loopholes and if there are outside factors which are deterring you from achieving your target, and you will have the power to address them. Instead of blaming others for not meeting your targets, even when it is true that they are responsible, by taking responsibility you are able to face the problem (e.g. you can approach your management and ask them to look into the matter).

Taking responsibility leads to taking action. When you do not take responsibility, you are merely tying your hands, rendering them useless. When you blame the economy for your failure to realize your dreams, you tie your hands instead of trying to get around the situation. It has long been known that even during an economic crisis there are those who can make a profit. Take responsibility instead of sitting back.

Taking responsibility is a step forward in breaking away from bad habits, and accepting responsibility gives you the power you need to take charge and develop good habits in place of bad habits.

5. Be in Control

We become slaves of our own habits because we give away control too easily. The reason why you are being led by your habit, like a dog on a leash, is because you have given up control. Get it in your mind that there is absolutely nothing making you do anything expect you. It is your life and you are in charge of it. It is true that many times we cannot stop the bad habits that form in our lives, but we can always control the urge that makes us behave in the manner we do. If you have a bad temper, you cannot really get rid of it, but you can choose to control it by taking a step back until you cool down before confronting the situation or person responsible for raising your ire.

When it comes to controlling our habits, we have a remote control at hand, which we can use but never do. Instead of mastering control, we behave as if we are on autopilot and perform solely as we have been program

It is high time you take back the control you have been giving away so easily. You are in charge of your life; master that control, and by doing so, you can also master your habits. Build self-control so that you are in a position to fight back the urge to do the wrong thing. Your body responds to what the mind is telling it to do, and nothing else. Mastering control is not an easy task but, over time, it can be accomplished.

Self-control can be quite easy to exercise if you avoid a bad habit altogether, but that may not be that easy. The sure way of exercising control is by having values. The question you need to ask yourself is, "What are my values?" It is only when you determine your standards, and the principles you wish to adhere to, that you will be able to master control. Having values makes us realize what is important in life and what we must be willing to sacrifice in order for us achieve our goals. If you want to run for a political office in your town, you will go to great lengths to keep your reputation intact, and you will do your best to avoid anything that can tarnish your image, which is exercising control.

Exercising control is all about looking at the bigger picture and knowing where you want to be, rather than looking at where you are now. If you want to lose weight, stop looking at how overweight you may be, and look instead at where you want to be, having a healthy, good-looking body. When you see what is at stake at the finish line, you can be motivated to lose weight and to stay motivated by sacrificing the things that keep you from getting to the finishing line.

6. Know What You Want Out of life.

Do you know what you want with your life? If the answer is no, then you have a problem. People who know what they want in life have habits that complement their goals, while on the other hand people who do not know what they want have a lot of bad habits. These habits go unchecked, because their habits are not in conflict with anything, whereas people who know what they want out of life are constantly in check of their habits. If your ambition in life is to become a lawyer, your habits will be in sync with your goal, thus you will study hard to obtain good grades and, more than likely, you will crush the bad habits that deter you from achieving this goal, such as laziness. Likewise, if your goal is to be promoted at work, the habits you will inherit are the ones that are pointed towards realizing this goal. You will make it a habit to be punctual, and will work hard to produce quality work so that you can realize your goal.

When you know what you want, it makes it easy for you to break free from bad habits that are counterproductive to reaching your goals. Thus, if you are serious about getting promoted at work, you will stop being late and producing mediocre results on the job.

Lacking direction in life arises as a result of not having a purpose. Do you know that there is a difference between living and existing? The difference is that people who exist do not have a purpose. They do not know what they want or what they are supposed to do, whilst people who truly live are the ones who have a purpose; they live to fulfill that purpose, they have goals and will do what is necessary to fulfill them. When you live for a purpose, you can easily get around bad habits because they prevent you from achieving what you want. The reason why you are bored and spending many hours on social networks may be attributed to your lack of purpose, and you lack purpose because you do not know what you want in life.

What you want out life is not always something that is grandiose. It can just be a matter of recognizing your immediate wants, like buying a car. When you know what you want, however simple or minor it might be, it is easy to let go of bad habits like excess spending. The fact that you have made the decision to buy a car, your money will not be spent on buying unnecessary things, but you learn to save until you have the sufficient amount to buy the car.

Knowing what you want in life should not be a difficult thing to decide. We are all different and want different things out of life. However, what you want out life should be that what makes you happy. Do not go fulfilling a purpose or dream that someone else has in mind for you, because that just leads to unhappiness. Start by writing down your goals, both short-term and long-term, and ask yourself, "If I fulfill these goals will I be happy?" When the answer is a resounding yes, you have found your purpose. That which makes you happy is a worthy cause to pursue.

Knowing your purpose helps you in forming good habits that enable you to fulfill your purpose such as working hard, excelling, confidence, healthy living, responsible behavior, time management, and many others. In the same regard, knowing your purpose and what you want in life will enable you to break away from bad habits.

Every day of your life should be about fulfilling and achieving something. When you do this, you put all of your energy into something positive. For example, reading an informative and inspirational article on healthy living is more constructive than surfing for pornographic material. When you wake up, wake up with a purpose and try to fulfill it. It might not be a purpose like going out to save the world, but at least it should be meaningful and be something that, at end of the day, you are proud of doing. You can wake up with the purpose of cleaning your house, or planting your garden. The fact of the matter is at the end of the day you have accomplished something, and your time was spent well. Choosing to go to the library to read as opposed to hanging out with the wrong crowd is a step towards fulfilling a purpose. It is essential to plan your day ahead.

7. Set Your Goals

There is a strong relationship between your goals and your habits. Setting goals gives your life a sense of direction. When you have direction, your mind, energy, time, and resources are focused on getting to your destination. Setting goals helps you to form habits that complement and support you in reaching your goal. Both long term and short term goals are the foundation you need to build good habits. If you have a short-term goal to lose twenty pounds in three months, you will automatically develop habits such as exercising regularly and healthy eating, so that you can achieve your goal. If your company wants to increase its profitability margin in the next quarter, it needs to set a goal to that effect. For the company to realize this profitability, there is need to form company habits that are directed to the achievement of this goal.

When setting goals, differentiate between short-term and long-term; determine what you want to achieve immediately and what you want to achieve in the future. There are short-term goals, which are linked to the achievement of long-term goals; hence you need to distinguish these goals.

Start by writing down all of your goals. Next, determine from your goal list your short-term and long-term goals. The short-term goals are the things you want to achieve in the present. These may include items like renovating your house, increasing clientele for your business, buying a car, or getting good grades on your exams. Long-term goals are the things you want to achieve in the future, or over a long period of time. Long-term goals include buying a house of your own, getting a law degree, or starting your own business venture.

After writing your goals, determine what you need to do to achieve that goal. Most of the goals you set for yourself cannot be achieved without you changing some aspects of your life. These aspects that need to change in your life include your habits. Changing a habit means that you replace a bad habit with a good habit that helps you in your journey towards achieving your goal. If your goal is buying a car at the end of the month, it means you have to replace the bad habit of overspending with the good habit of saving. Similarly, if you want a good grade on your exam, you are going have to get rid of laziness and start to work hard.

Goals are the catalyst to habit formation; you cannot aim to achieve your goals without making reasonable changes to the way you do things. If a company wants to make a turnaround, it has to change the way it does things in the first place. When you set goals for yourself, changing of your current habit follows, and when you cut out a bad habit, a good habit grows in its place.

However, for you to build good habits, merely setting goals is not enough. You also need determination and the commitment to achieve the goal. When you are determined and committed, you are in a position to change so that you achieve something. Commitment helps you with sticking and adhering to your new habits.

Do not start by setting goals that are hard to achieve or are unreasonable. Always remember that a journey of a thousand miles starts with the first step. The first step is setting goals that you know you have the capacity to achieve. Start with minor things that you never get around to, like working out or planting an herb garden.

Chapter 3 Habit 8-14

1. Start Thinking Positive

Positive thinking is important in building habits that make us successful. If our habits make us the people we are, then by removing negativity from our lives we are able to positively influence the way we go about doing things. People carry on with bad habits because they fill their lives with negativity. If you are always negative about yourself, you will always have the "cannot do" habit. When you think negatively about yourself and your abilities, it results in you not being able to get rid of your bad habits. Negative thinking limits you, but when you think positively, you will realize that the possibilities of what you can do are limitless. When you think positively, you able to realize that transformation is possible and you can do just about anything. We keep bad habits with us because there is a lot of negativity that surrounds us. For instance, a lot of people procrastinate on achieving their goals because they are simply afraid of the outcome.

When you think positively, you can do just about anything. You are able to picture what you want. If your dream is to be a successful entrepreneur, be positive about it and realize that there is no force other than yourself that can stop you from achieving this dream.

When you think positively, you start to build habits necessary for success. Positive thinking is all about "can" and "will," so use these terms in your vocabulary rather than the negative terms like "cannot." If you want positivity in your life, surround yourself with positive influences. Make it your mission to be around positive people, people who have done something, and people who can inspire you. If you want to achieve body fitness, find the right people who have the same agenda as yours. If you want to get good grades at school, do not expect to find positive influence from high school dropouts that spend their time doing nothing. Instead, be around people who have achieved good grades, or who are working hard to get them.

2. Choose the Right Environment

The environment plays a significant role in shaping people. A lot of people are who they are because of the environment they were brought up in. The environment can make or break you. In the business world, the issue of environment is understood quite well. Companies spend a lot of money, so as to gain perspective on the environment. Environmental analysis is done in business to obtain a better understanding of the forces at work. Without this analysis, the company might fail. The same applies to life situations in the way that our environment shapes us. Imagine what it is like when you want to eat healthy foods, but the environment you are in is full of people who enjoy junk foods.

Your habits are connected to your environment. For example, you may eat cupcakes every day because you live opposite to the bakery, or you speak too loudly because you work in a noisy club. The environment influences most of our habits; our daily routine is as a result of what we have around us. You watch television all day because you have the television in your home, you spend all day surfing the Internet because you have a wireless connection, or you read because you have a library in your home. All of these habits develop because of the environment. For a person to be able to build good habits, they need an environment that is in line with their goals. For example, if you want career growth, you need to work for a company that values employee development. Place yourself in the right environment, because the environment has a huge impact on us on both subconscious and conscious levels.

Look for the environment that is right for you. The environment you choose helps you to form the right habits. If you want to achieve something, then you must be in the right place. The environment is not always about your location; it can mean the crowd of people that surrounds you as well.

3. Remove Temptation

If you want to build good habits, you must remove the temptations around you. If you are looking to develop a habit of healthy eating, the first step you need to take is to remove all unhealthy foods from your refrigerator and cupboards. If you have a habit of watching pornography every night and you wish to stop, you should remove all of the pornographic material. When you remove temptations, you are manipulating the habit formation cycle. You can easily break a habit if you remove temptation, because temptation is the trigger that makes us engage in bad habits. When you get rid of pornographic magazines, you are removing the trigger that makes you read and look at pornography.

If you want to form a study habit, remove the temptation that stops you from studying, which may be things like the television in your room or your phone. Removing temptations is not always easy, because most of the things that tempt us in life disable us from exercising our willpower over them.

When dealing with temptation, it is important to identify first and foremost the reason behind the temptation. It is only when we identify the reason behind the temptation that we may be able to have the ammunition to conquer it. In the habit formation process, temptation can be identified as the cue. If you want to break away from a bad habit, then you should fight the edge to engage in the routine. If you have a habit of constantly fidgeting in your chair and you want to stop doing this, you should identify the cue that triggers you to fidget. The reason may be that you are bored or you are just nervous. Understanding the cue or temptation gives us more insight to the habit. Behind every bad habit, there is always a bigger problem that causes us to behave in the manner we do. In the example on fidgeting, fidgeting is a minor problem; the major problem is the reason behind the habit. You fidget only because you are bored or you are feeling nervous.

By facing our temptations, we are able to develop a good habit in order to conquer that temptation. When you feel tempted to reach out for a carbonated drink in the refrigerator and fight that edge by reaching for bottled water, you would have effectively conquered the temptation. If you do this every time, eventually it is going to develop into a good habit.

4. Start Taking Action

The reason you never get around to doing anything in your life is simply because you do not do anything. Thinking of what you want to do and spending time fantasizing about it will not bring anything to your doorstep. Saying, "I am going to quit smoking" is not the same thing as actually stopping to smoke. Saying, "I am going to start exercising regularly" is not the same as actually excising. Much of our time is spent talking about what we want and what we are going to do instead of actually doing what we have in mind. The world would be a better place for everybody if people actually got to do the things they talk about, but sadly, we spend our energy and time daydreaming.

If you want to, nothing stops you from getting what you want. We hold on to bad habits even when we know that they are bad for us, because instead of stopping, we want to stop. No one ever said breaking bad habits was easy. The fact that you have become accustomed to that pattern of behavior makes it very hard for you to stop even when you know it's bad. When you say, "I want to stop," it means that you have taken the first step. It is now registered in your mind that you should stop. Take the next step, which is the action. We all know that bad habits take time to let go, but taking the first tentative steps to giving up your habit ensures that, in time, you can fully let go of the habit.

If you want to quit smoking, start by reducing the number of cigarettes you smoke in a day. As you gradually decrease the cigarettes you smoke, in time you can completely stop. If you want to get around to reading the best classic novels collection, you can save a great deal of time and energy by simply reading the first page of one classic novel? If you want to achieve something, you should do it. Do not spend time talking about wanting to start running 5 kilometers every morning; rather, spur yourself to action by running around the block of your neighborhood.

If you want to develop a good habit, then do it. If you can imagine it, you can do it. There is nothing that can stop you from achieving what you want. If you want to be a doctor, what is stopping you? Lacking action is our greatest failure in life.

Get out of the habit of spending time thinking or saying what you want. Everything in life will seem easier when you start doing it. It's like embarking on a long journey by foot; when you think about the journey, it seems impossible, but the moment you start walking, the distance gets shorter, and getting to your destination is no longer impossible. If you want to be happy rather than spending time talking about it, start by doing at least one thing that makes you happy.

5. Face Your Fear

Fear keeps you in a box; you are unable to go anywhere because you live in fear. Fear holds you back, because you cannot move forward, so you stay in the same position hoping that your fears will pass. The reality is, they rarely do unless you confront them. Many bad habits can arise as a result of fear, and many times you may not realize that you do the things you do because you live in fear. The first step you need to take in facing your fears is to recognize and identify them. Make a list of the things you fear, which is the first step in confrontation. When you list your fears, you may actually realize how some of them are so trivial and irrational. What you will have left are rational fears, and from them you can establish which fears you can deal with and the ones beyond your control.

The next step you need to take in confronting your fear is thinking about it. When you seriously think about your fear in a small measure, you are confronting it. Do not dwell your thoughts on how terrified you get, but dwell your thoughts on the object of your fear. Think about the things your fear stops you from achieving, and also think about the negative things that have been caused by your fear. Think about the things you have lost because of your fear and what you have gained because of that fear.

The next step in confronting your fear is making a decision on what you want to do. Decide for yourself if you want to remain in fear and lose out, or if you want to face your fear and gain something. Most of our fears are baseless; we fear things that we have not yet actually done, and as a result, most of our habits are because of fear. Fear does more harm than good.

6. Motivate Yourself with Rewards

We rarely do anything without the necessary motivation to fuel us in any activity we undertake. In habit formation, the element of motivation is ever present. Motivation is a drive, which can send us in search for the object of our desire. The reason we hold onto bad habits, even when we know they do more harm than good, is because we are motivated to indulge in the routine. For instance, the feeling you get after watching porn is the motivation that makes you watch it in the first place.

As long as you find the motivation, there is nothing that keeps you from indulging in your routine. The key in developing good habits is in finding the motivation that appeals to you, so that you get more into the habit. The prospect of beautiful, flawless skin is a motivation to drinking water. Being able to fit into your favorite pair of jeans is motivation to jog more often. Obtaining a scholarship is also motivation to study hard. If you want to build good habits, make the habit attainable for you by associating the habit with appealing rewards. For instance, flawless skin is more appealing than water; hence, instead of focusing on the habit of drinking water, you can focus on the reward of flawless skin. The fact that at the end of the day your skin will be beautiful and flawless is your motivation to make the habit of drinking water stick.

The major problem that we have when it comes to breaking free from bad habits and replacing them with good habits is simply that bad habits are more enjoyable than good habits. Also, the reward obtained from a bad habit is immediate, as opposed to the reward derived from a good habit, which is mostly realized over time. Simply put, drinking a glass of coke is more rewarding than drinking a glass of water. With a glass of coke, you get to quench your thirst while at the same time enjoying the refreshing taste, whereas with water, you just quench your thirst, but there is no enjoyment. However, in the long run, drinking water has its ultimate rewards.

To overcome this problem, it is important that you first take time to consider the potential benefits of the habit that you want to develop. If you want to develop a habit of punctuality, you must first look at the benefits to be derived from being punctual. If being punctual makes you do all your errands on time and leaves you with extra time on your hands, use that benefit as a motivation to develop the habit and make it stick. For each and every good habit you want to develop, use the same exercise of evaluating its benefit/reward and using that as motivation to keep you hooked on the habit.

7. Take One Step at a Time/One Habit at a Time

Logically, it is best to develop one good habit at a time. Developing one good habit that actually sticks is better than developing many good habits all at once and failing to make any one of them stick over time. Keep in mind that you are a work in progress; you do more if you take it step-by-step rather than completely trying to transform yourself. No one is perfect, hence you should not try to transform yourself into a robot that is programmed to perfection; imperfections are what make us human.

Think of the area or aspect in your life that is holding you back from achieving your goals. This is where you should start to develop a habit that you know can conquer your weakness. Another way is to find at least one bad habit that is affecting your lifestyle. Develop a good habit that helps you transform that aspect of your life. If excess spending is causing havoc in your life, it is time to break free from this habit by working around it and developing a habit of saving money. When you focus on one habit, it entails that all of your energy is focused on one objective, and you are more likely to see it through.

Change is a process; you cannot transform overnight. It is essential to take small steps towards achieving a goal. Do not overwhelm yourself by trying to change a lot of things in your lifestyle. Changing your lifestyle starts by letting go of at least one habit.

Chapter -4 Habit-15-21

8. Piggyback with Existing Habits

This support system can be very effective if you want to develop good habits that you can actually stick to. Piggyback a desired habit with the good habits you already have. In simpler terms, piggybacking habits is a process whereby you put together a habit that you desire to have with another habit that you already have. If you want to develop a habit of reading the bible every night and you already have a habit of praying every night, you should put the bible close by so that after praying you read the bible. Likewise, if you want to develop a habit of flossing before you go to bed and are already in the habit of brushing your teeth, stack these two habits together. Put your toothbrush together with the floss and let it gradually develop into a habit. Piggybacking habits makes it much easier to bring new habits into the fold instead of just developing a new habit from nowhere. Piggybacking habits makes the process of adapting to new habits easy and effective, because you are not disrupting your system; you are simply integrating new and old habits. This ensures that the newly found habits stick with you.

Piggybacking works where there is a relationship between the existing and the desired habit. This is regarded as the easiest way of developing habits. So make a list of all your existing good habits and another list of the habits you desire to have. Then, look between the two lists so you can find the ones that are linked and start piggybacking.

9. Get Organized

The truth of the matter is that you cannot achieve anything if you are not organized. If you lack order in your life, you never get to do anything. Having stacks of things that you never get to do is typical when you lack organization. Before you try a hand at transforming yourself, first and foremost put your house in order. It is impossible to transform your life when you do not know where to begin or which area needs critical attention.

Many people, when thinking about organization, think of putting a room order, organizing a desk, or filing receipts, when in actually the first place you start organizing your life is mentally. Many people have mental war going on in their mind, meaning they have a lot of things they want to do but do not know how to go about it. This is the scenario when you try different activities all at once and eventually you do not get to complete even one activity.

Get out of this mental war and start planning your life in a systematic way. We know that you want to do great things and achieve greatness, but you have to take it one step at a time. It is okay to dream big, but you must first start small. Do not congest your mind with more than it can take.
Create a, "to do list" written in order of the things that need to be done, and make a mental note. Do not over plan or take on more than you can bear. Start with an area you know really needs your attention that you can no longer choose to neglect. Our

lives are not picture perfect, so finding a gray area in your life is not too hard.

Develop an understanding of this gray area, and from there make a note to change. Lastly, take the required action.

10. Measure your Progress

Measuring your progress is an important trait to habit building; you need to know how you are doing and if you are on the right track. Habits take time to develop; you cannot develop a habit in a single day. It takes time for a habit to sink in before they can become automatic. Establish where you started and where you are now, and determine if you have made progress. Measuring your progress brings you to full awareness of what needs to be done.

Habits take their time to develop, so you need to know if the habit you are trying to build is taking root. When you measure your progress and realize what needs to be done, you can establish a way forward.

11. Form a Support Group

Never underestimate the power of a support group. If you truly want to develop good habits that will stick with you in the long run, you need to be around people who are supportive. A support groups makes you stay positive and gives you encouragement to move forward. This is why support groups like Alcoholics Anonymous are effective; because they are full of people who want to achieve something. If you want to obtain good grades, you need to be part of a support group that has the same goal as yours. In the same way, if you want to lose weight, take part in a group with the same objective as yours.

19. Maintain Consistencies

If you want to get to the finish line, maintain consistencies. Change your thinking and attitude and be realistic. Don't generalize your plan for today; you have to be more specific to what you really want. You need to have willpower to do this. Being consistent is synonymous with being supplied by a continuous and steady amount of effort to achieve something positive and something good. You have to agree and follow ways you knew would make yourself satisfied, but it should not be limited to just self-satisfaction.

Consistency should not be contaminated with logical contradictions, either; otherwise, you will be misled into believing that everything is fine, but in reality, something is not quite right. One example is when you think you are going to eat healthy food every day and promise yourself that you will never eat junk foods. You better be consistent to follow this habit, and do not go for other options. So, you better assess everything if you are being consistent, by evaluating an unchanging approach and apply fairly well what you have in your mind. This reasoning will seldom give you inaccurate answers to everyday query, and a second opinion from a friend, your spouse (if you have one), a colleague, or our ever-reliable parents could be of great help. They could be your witness if you are being consistent every day. Parents are primarily the best people that can assess your development of good habits. When you live with or near them, they can easily identify the changes. As they are around since you are born and up to the time you become independent, they are there. They are like the "coaches" that could appraise your performance, good or bad. And a good and responsible coach can see almost anything in a ballgame.

The second person or people that could give reliable round up with your habit changes are your siblings. Like our parents, they are also our companions when we are growing up, and they can easily spot those changes. The people that surround you have the greatest part in building your habits that could make you good and consistent. You could not be your own critic, because people tend to protect themselves, which enables them to fall beyond his or her consistency until it is too late to reform. So, being consistent is really a big issue, but it can be addressed. Follow these simple steps and you can never be wrong. Simple steps need simple solutions.

Behaving in a similar way every day entails consistency, and any good habit that you would like to achieve would be better off by allowing yourself to flow with the changing times. Some of the greatest achievers of our generation pursued habits, and they never stopped afterwards. Like Bill Gates (Microsoft founder) and

Steven Spielberg (Hollywood filmmaker) who were wide readers since their young age. They read books, journals, and everything concerning their respective fields. Look at them now. They have created their respective empires worth billions of dollars. They never stopped reading, and they still rake in the gold. Their habit of reading enabled them to earn knowledge and put them into action and, consequently, earned them well.

20. Give it Time

You are not going to get the results you want right then and there. As the Divine Creator Himself took time to create life and light on earth, a wound takes time to heal, and, like a plant that takes a period of time and nourishment to grow, it is the same as building a habit. It really takes quite some time to develop a habit subconsciously; you should not solely rely on time to make it happen. Relying solely on time is like waiting for the moon to fall. You have to act and comprehend the steps to attain one.

Ample time need not be too brief, though. This book's presented techniques, which could be done in one month, require too much patience and tons of precision. Why precision? Do you have to measure anything? Certainly, yes! Brief timing means a lot. When we said timing, we meant a whole lot of attention to detail. However, this will not make you like a college student trying to solve a problem in math or to spell an alien word that nobody knows exists. We just mean events happening to you every day, and only you can make the difference. Give it time to grow and you will be surprise of the consequences. As we have said earlier, change has to start somewhere, and time will bring it to life.

If you are a struggling entrepreneur and you want to win clients, you could develop a habit of not talking when not asked, you could wait for the right timing and precise words to be laid in order for the client to earn your trust and thus, earning you more. Time is of the essence, really, and learning habits to make you nice to everybody makes sense. Basically, if you have no time, then you had better make it. It will save you more of it in the near future. Ordinary people want something extraordinary, and extraordinary people want something ordinary. Isn't that ironic? But it does happen. So, if you are an ordinary person, achieve the extraordinary, change habits, then if you achieve what you were dreaming of, you would surely seek the ordinary, as this will make you feel fulfilled. That is the cycle of life. Nobody gets satisfaction; only change could satisfy anyone. You are bound to commit satisfaction when you are able to complete the cycle, and then you will realize that you are still alive and kicking.

Steve Jobs once said, "My favorite things in life don't cost any money, it is really clear that the most precious resource we all have is time." He was truly right when he said that.

21. Redefine Yourself

After you have weighed all the possibilities of the techniques in building good habits, transforming them into reality is never truly easy, because you have to sacrifice something. Simply put, disregard all old habits you want to erase. Thirty days of transformation is really quite a miraculous feat. But for those who want changes at this period, remember that it could be realized; you have only to make it clear and compromise what you really want. You just have to describe your scope or make clear statements about what you want to achieve during this brief period. If you could take them all at one time, fine, and if not, then you are better to set other habit transformation for the future, or schedule them firmly for some other time.

But how could you really redefine yourself? One possible way is to let go of the past. Does it help to carry the past every day? If not, then you had better let go of them, and we mean right now! All of us probably had bitter experiences from the past: High school bullies, being dumped by someone you loved, chain smoking, not being promoted despite working ten straight years at a company, becoming an alcoholic, or any other tragedy.

Take some deep breaths and concentrate, and then break the chain. It would make you relax and feel freer in your lives. Start to move on and set the timeline. Do you believe you could establish a set of standards that you could not turn your back to? Redefining yourself is not a ton of gravel that is so heavy, it is better to be sure you have the guts and do not depend on anyone to achieve and carry the weight, but you can use ideas and support others thrown at your doorstep, as long as you can learn how to handle them.

The power of the mind cannot be deceived. If you have willpower, change is inevitable, and it is desirable to change something you do not want to explode in the future. You cannot disguise your true longing for life; you could change those bad habits and these techniques will give you ideas others may not know about.

Determining how you cope with changes in your life will make you stronger and focused. That feeling of fulfilment may bring positive vibes that will surely boost your desire to enhance whatever habit you choose to pursue. You could defy nature by undergoing habit-forming activities not typically seen in a short period of time just to make everything realized. Furthermore, the things you value, including both the principles and personality traits could lead to a positive transformation, and you could stick to them no matter what.

When everything is set in place, the journey to change should begin. And it is more likely to be today. Do not delay; you can start now, now that you know our techniques.

Conclusion

So, we arrived at the formidable moment when you are keen on pursuing some nice habits to make you more desirable to others, not necessarily to make them love you, but just like that; to be nice. The laid techniques on building some amazing and likeable habits will somehow make it possible, and mind you, at an early time. As we have learned that any habit is unique to everyone, like a thumbprint, where all human thumbs have the same features and textures, but their prints are distinctly their own. We are all different.

The step-by-step techniques listed here could be figured out once one was open enough to see the realization. Skipping one technique is not advisable, as this could ruin all of your efforts, and you could end up having achieved nothing. You might not accept a "better luck next time" proposition, because the best time is today, and there could be no other time. Once you put forth the momentum, it is best not to stop. Do not put breaks on the momentum; it might disengage the building blocks of constructing the pathway to success.

You must really define what you want, and changing things to make you grow better and becomes successful, not unlike the billionaires that we admired and the celebrities we idolize. They may not be so hard to duplicate after all. They were like you once, and they might have come from a much more miserable life than you have now, but their pathways were probably paved the way you are now trying to pave yours. You must choose your own path, not anyone else; it is just you. You could make your own cake, and you could eat it, or save some for tomorrow. But the decision is yours to make.

Forming good habits and then running for them successfully may not give you pleasure later, as you would long for another round of changes, but at least you know now how to handle those difficult task of attaining habits to advance your interest. Pleasure would be so sweet to attain and changing it would be so easily achievable the second time around. So brace yourself, and apply the things you have learned by doing these 21 fabulous techniques of building good habits in transforming your life in just 30 days.